THE BEST OF
Fred

Rupert Fawcett invented Fred nine years ago
and both their lives have taken off since then.
Rupert has got married and become a father while
Fred has become something of a star with books
and merchandise in several countries.

Fred's past life is documented in Rupert's eight
previous books: *Fred*, *More Fred*, *The Extraordinary
World of Fred*, *The Continued Adventures of Fred*,
Carry on Fred, *At Home with Fred*, *Pure Fred*, and
The One and Only Fred. Fred can also be seen in
the *Mail on Sunday*.

The Best of Fred contains 185 favourite
Fred illustrations depicting Fred's zany life with
the good-natured Penelope and ever-present
black cat, Anthony.

Also by Rupert Fawcett published by Headline

CARRY ON FRED

AT HOME WITH FRED

PURE FRED

THE ONE AND ONLY FRED

THE BEST OF Fred

Rupert Fawcett

HEADLINE

First published in 1998
by HEADLINE BOOK PUBLISHING

10 9 8 7 6 5 4 3 2 1

ISBN 0 7472 7607 2

Printed and bound in Italy by
Canale & C. S.p.A

HEADLINE BOOK PUBLISHING
A division of Hodder Headline PLC
338 Euston Road
London NW1 3BH

FRED AND PENELOPE SPENT ANOTHER
EVENING IN THE FAST LANE

WHERE PIP'S SOCKS WERE CONCERNED
THE KEY WORD WAS 'CAUTION`

FRED LIKED TO SPEND HIS WEEKENDS
RELAXING ON THE GOLF COURSE

PENELOPE WAS DETERMINED NOT TO BE
PUT OFF BY HER FIRST EXPERIENCE
OF BAKING

IT SEEMED A CRUEL IRONY THAT
TINY WAS THE ONLY PERSON UNABLE
TO ATTEND HIS OWN BIRTHDAY PARTY

IT WAS ANOTHER OF FRED'S
MECHANIC DREAMS

CHRISTMAS WAS CELEBRATED WITH ONE OF
FRED'S FAMOUS INDOOR BARBECUES

PIP HAD ALWAYS BEEN A BIG
FAN OF PENELOPE'S SOUPS

FRED ALWAYS HATED IT WHEN PENELOPE
POPPED OUT FOR A CUP OF TEA
WITH THE NEIGHBOURS

MR AND MRS NESBIT NEVER TIRED OF
HEARING ABOUT FRED AND PENELOPE'S
1973 HOLIDAY IN SPAIN

PENELOPE WAS A GREAT BELIEVER
IN THE POWER OF PRAYER

ALL FRED HAD EVER KNOWN ABOUT HIS SECOND COUSIN WAS THAT HE WAS 'SOMETHING BIG IN THE CITY'

FRED HAD NEVER BEEN A BIG
FAN OF THE DAWN CHORUS

SEEING HIS BOOK IN THE SHOPS FOR THE
FIRST TIME GAVE FRED A TREMENDOUS
FEELING OF ACCOMPLISHMENT

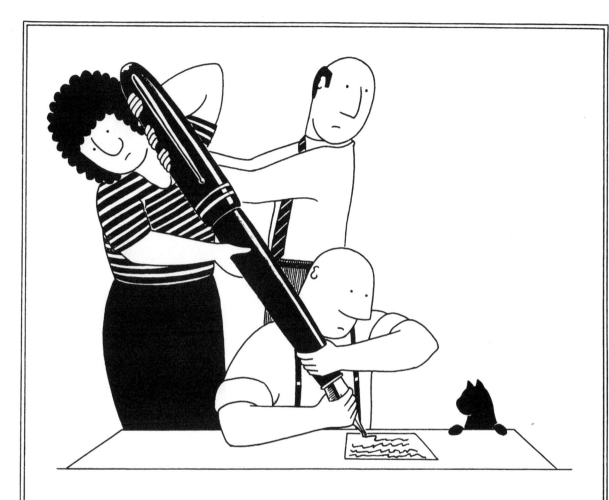

FRED WAS EXPERIENCING SOME
DIFFICULTY WITH HIS NEW
'ECONOMY SIZE' PEN

FRED WAS STILL TRYING TO COME TO
TERMS WITH THE LOSS OF TEDDY

WHILE PENELOPE PREPARED THE DINNER
FRED LOOKED AFTER THE GUESTS

ONCE A MONTH FRED WOULD GET
TOGETHER WITH HIS FISHING PALS

FRED CERTAINLY KNEW HOW TO
TURN PENELOPE ON

YEARS OF EXPERIENCE HAD TAUGHT
FRED TO STAND WELL BACK WHILE
PENELOPE PREPARED HER BREAKFAST

FRED COULD ALWAYS TELL WHEN
THE GOLDFISH WERE ARGUING

AS PART OF HER NEW FITNESS PROGRAMME
PENELOPE WATCHED HER JANE FONDA
AEROBICS VIDEO EVERY DAY WITHOUT FAIL

FRED WAS QUITE HAPPY TO HAVE PENELOPE'S
MOTHER TO STAY FOR CHRISTMAS SO LONG
AS SHE WAS ON HER MEDICATION

SUCH WAS THE POWER OF FRED'S IMAGINATION
THAT SO FAR AS HE WAS CONCERNED HE
<u>WAS</u> THOMAS THE TANK ENGINE

AT LAST THE MAN ARRIVED
ABOUT THE DAMP

FRED HAD ALWAYS BEEN SUSPICIOUS
ABOUT PENELOPE'S SO-CALLED
'AEROBICS CLASSES'

PENELOPE WAS BUSY ACCUMULATING
EVIDENCE FOR HER NOISE POLLUTION
COMPENSATION CLAIM

THE REACTION TO FRED'S HOMEMADE
LEMONADE WAS UNIFORM

AFTER MONTHS OF PREPARATION
SHOOTING FINALLY GOT UNDERWAY ON
'FRED — THE INGROWING TOE NAIL'

'IT'S THE PRIME MINISTER AGAIN',
SIGHED PENELOPE

FRED SPENT THE AFTERNOON WORKING ON
HIS CHRISTMAS MESSAGE TO THE NATION

FRED AND PENELOPE SPENT THE
AFTERNOON ENGROSSED IN THEIR
CHRISTMAS PRESENTS

FRED SPENT THE AFTERNOON RESEARCHING HIS
FORTHCOMING BOOK, 'ONE THOUSAND WAYS
TO EAT A FLAPJACK'

FRED WAS BECOMING INCREASINGLY
CONCERNED ABOUT PENELOPE'S EYESIGHT

FRED WAS TIRED OF HEARING PIP
WHINGEING ABOUT THE BUNGEE JUMP

FRED'S DINNER GUESTS MADE THE
MISTAKE OF ARRIVING FIVE
MINUTES LATE

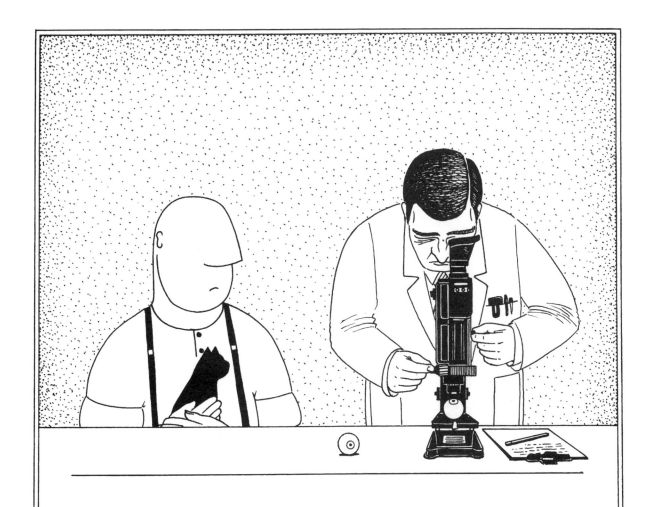

FRED ALWAYS HATED HAVING
HIS EYES TESTED

FRED HAD AN UNINTERRUPTED
VIEW OF PIP'S CAR BEING
WHEEL-CLAMPED

FRED'S LATEST INVENTION WAS DESIGNED
TO DO THE WORK OF TEN MEN

FRED FINALLY GOT LUCKY DOWN
AT THE JOB CENTRE

FRED HAD NEVER BEEN WHAT YOU
COULD CALL A 'KEEN' GARDENER

FRED WENT TO GREAT LENGTHS TO TRACE
HIS OLD SCHOOL MASTER 'SIX-OF-THE-BEST'
SIMPSON AND INVITE HIM ROUND TO LUNCH

FRED SEEMED UNABLE TO CONTAIN HIS
REACTION TO PIP'S NEW 'CARDIE'

IT WAS FRED AND PENELOPE'S
FIRST EXPERIENCE OF PET-SWAPPING

EVERY SUMMER FRED AND PENELOPE
LIKED TO GET AWAY FROM IT ALL

FROM TIME TO TIME FRED WOULD
TAKE THE MORE ADVENTUROUS
ROUTE TO THE NEWSAGENT

FRED'S LATEST INVENTION TOOK THE SWEAT OUT OF BACK-SCRATCHING

FRED AND PIP ALWAYS GREETED
EACH OTHER WITH THE SECRET
HANDSHAKE OF B.L.O.B.B. ; THE
BRITISH LEAGUE OF BALD BLOKES

PENELOPE'S KEEP-FIT CAMPAIGN
GOT OFF TO A GENTLE START

FRED AND PENELOPE TOOK IT IN
TURNS TO GO TO THE SHOPS

SUNDAY WAS SPENT TESTING
FRED'S LATEST INVENTION, THE
WALK 'N' PAINT CEILING ROLLER

'THEY CAN KEEP THEIR SEAN CONNERYS AND HARRISON FORDS', SIGHED PENELOPE

FRED HAD AN UNQUENCHABLE
THIRST FOR ADVENTURE

BOB AND PENELOPE ALWAYS GOT
VERY TORVILL AND DEAN ABOUT
THE MILK BILL

FRED LOVED ENTERTAINING

SATURDAY NIGHT
WAS LOTTERY NIGHT

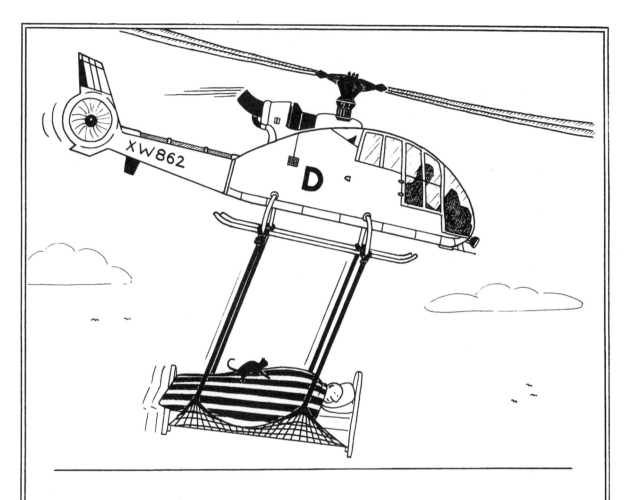

READING 'HOW TO GO TO WORK WITHOUT
GETTING OUT OF BED' HAD BEEN A
LIFE-CHANGING EXPERIENCE FOR FRED

PENELOPE COULDN'T WAIT TO SEE
WHAT FRED HAD PREPARED FOR
HER SURPRISE BIRTHDAY DINNER

PENELOPE REALISED SHE HAD BEEN
A FOOL TO LET FRED CHOOSE THE
HOLIDAY DESTINATION

FRED WAS DISMAYED TO DISCOVER
HIS NEWSAGENT HAD COMPLETELY
SOLD OUT OF 'WHAT TROUSERS'?

FRED AND PENELOPE
MADE A GREAT TEAM

FRED HAD VARIOUS WAYS OF
GETTING RID OF UNWANTED GUESTS

APPARENTLY MR NESBIT'S DOCTOR
HAD RECOMMENDED NO MORE THAN
ONE GLASS OF BEER PER DAY

FRED FINALLY REACHED A DECISION
CONCERNING THE CUCKOO CLOCK

FRED HAD A KEEN INTEREST IN
MODERN ENGLISH LITERATURE

'THIS IS THE LAST TIME WE
TRAVEL SUPER-ECONOMY',
SPAT PENELOPE

FRED SPENT MONTHS RESEARCHING HIS FORTHCOMING BOOK, 'HOW TO EAT A SPAGHETTI BOLOGNESE WITHOUT USING YOUR HANDS'

PENELOPE ALWAYS PUT A
LOT OF THOUGHT INTO
FRED'S CHRISTMAS PRESENT

FRED HAD NEVER SHARED PENELOPE'S
ENTHUSIASM FOR CHRISTMAS SHOPPING

'IT LOOKS LIKE A SIMPLE CASE OF
ONE MINCE PIE TOO MANY,'
CONCLUDED THE DOCTOR

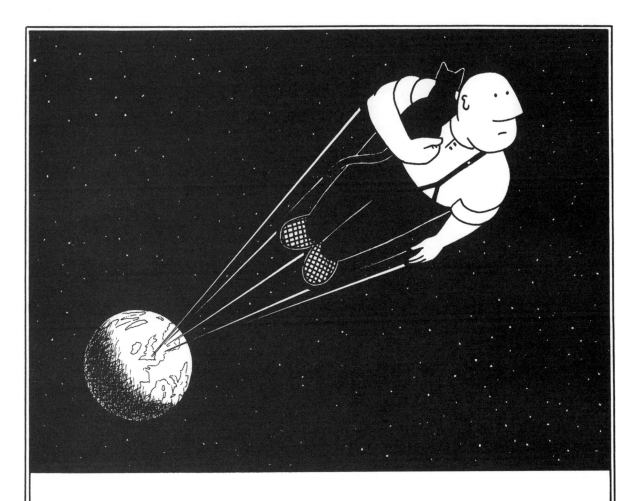

FRED REALISED HE HAD BEEN A FOOL
TO UNDERESTIMATE THE POWER
OF PENELOPE'S KICK

IT WAS TIME FOR FRED'S INTERVIEW
DOWN AT THE JOB CENTRE

PENELOPE ASSURED FRED THAT
HE WOULD GROW TO LOVE
THE NEW DECOR

AS USUAL THERE WAS SOME
DISAGREEMENT OVER WHO SHOULD
HAVE THE LAST JAFFA CAKE

PENELOPE'S BREAKFAST ARRIVED AT
THE SAME TIME EVERY MORNING

IT WAS TO BE PENELOPE'S
FIRST AND LAST ATTEMPT
AT ROCK CAKES

PENELOPE COULDN'T WAIT TO SEE
FRED'S REACTION TO HER SENSUOUS
NEW PERFUME, 'SEDUCTION IN PARIS'

FRED COULDN'T HELP FEELING
THAT PIP WAS OVER-REACTING
TO HIS £10 LOTTERY WIN

FRED FOUND THE NEW WINDOW CLEANER
A LITTLE OVER-FAMILIAR

FRED SPENT CHRISTMAS EVE
PREPARING FOR THE ARRIVAL
OF HIS IN-LAWS

THERE WERE MOMENTS ON THE
CYCLING HOLIDAY WHEN PENELOPE
WISHED FRED COULD PEDAL JUST
THAT LITTLE BIT HARDER

FRED AND PENELOPE LOVED TO
EXPERIMENT WITH NEW
PAINT TECHNIQUES

FRED HAD FALLEN OUT WITH
THE NEIGHBOURS AGAIN

PENELOPE COULDN'T HELP THINKING
THE CHIPPENDALES AUDITION
WOULD END IN TEARS

AFTER TEA PENELOPE SAT DOWN
WITH HER KNITTING WHILE FRED
GOT ON WITH A SPOT OF D.I.Y.

FRED OFTEN DREAMED OF DESIGNING
A GOLF COURSE OF HIS OWN

FRED WAS THRILLED THAT THE
LOCAL AMATEUR DRAMATIC SOCIETY
HAD FINALLY GIVEN HIM A PART

FRED AND PENELOPE ALWAYS
PROVIDED THEIR GUESTS WITH
AFTER-DINNER ENTERTAINMENT

FRED HAD HEARD THAT PIP
WAS FOND OF FAST FOOD

FRED AND PENELOPE LIKED TO END
·THE DAY WITH A NICE GLASS
OF WARM MILK

PIP WISHED HE HAD NEVER AGREED TO
HELP FRED WITH THE PRUNING

FRED AND PENELOPE LOVED TO GET
OUT INTO THE COUNTRY AND
STRETCH THEIR LEGS

PENELOPE COULDN'T HELP FEELING
THAT FRED WASN'T ENTERING
INTO THE TRUE SPIRIT OF
THE ADVENTURE HOLIDAY

'NO PEACE FOR THE WICKED',
SIGHED FRED

FOR MANY YEARS FRED'S SECRET SUNDAY
AFTERNOON NAPS WENT UNDETECTED

FRED AND PENELOPE'S GUESTS
COULD ALWAYS BE SURE OF
A WARM WELCOME

EVERYBODY WAS ASKED TO WAIT
PATIENTLY FOR THEIR TURN WITH
THE SCATTER CUSHIONS

HAVING BEEN UNABLE TO OBTAIN A LION,
FRED SETTLED FOR THE SLIGHTLY LESS
DANGEROUS PURSUIT OF SLUG-TAMING

PENELOPE WAS RELIEVED THAT FRED
HAD AT LAST AGREED TO ATTEND
'ROAD-RAGE' COUNSELLING

FRED DERIVED IMMENSE PLEASURE
FROM SITTING IN THE BATH FOR
EXTENDED PERIODS AND WATCHING
EVERYTHING GO WRINKLY

IF FRED AND PENELOPE'S FIRST B+B
CUSTOMER HAD ONE COMPLAINT, IT
WOULD SIMPLY BE THAT THEY WERE
TRYING A LITTLE TOO HARD

FRED HAD PROMISED TO GET
MR AND MRS NESBIT HOME IN TIME
FOR THE ARCHERS

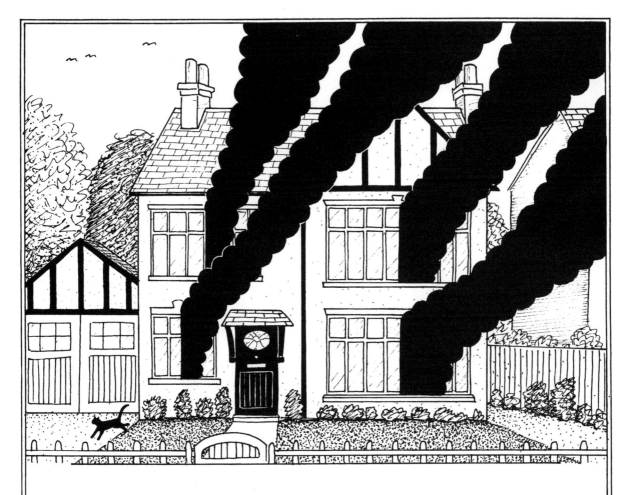

AFTER LUNCH FRED TREATED HIS
CHRISTMAS GUESTS TO AN INDOOR
FIREWORK DISPLAY

PENELOPE WAS BEGINNING TO WISH
SHE HAD NEVER BOUGHT FRED
THE CAMCORDER

HAVING GROWN BORED WITH SLUG-TAMING
FRED DECIDED TO TRY HIS HAND
AT WORM-CHARMING

WHAT PENELOPE LIKED MOST ABOUT
LIFE WITH FRED WAS THAT THERE WAS
NEVER A DULL MOMENT

FRED AND PIP WERE THE KINDA GUYS
THAT LIKED TO WORK HARD
AND PLAY HARD

FRED AND PENELOPE SPENT
MANY HAPPY EVENINGS RE-LIVING
THEIR HONEYMOON IN VENICE

ALTHOUGH EVERYBODY LOVED FRED
THEY EACH HAD THEIR OWN
FAVOURITE BIT

PENELOPE FOUND HERSELF WONDERING
WHY SHE HADN'T SIMPLY GONE TO
HER CHIROPODIST APPOINTMENT
BY BUS

WE CALL IT 'ACUTE SOAP ADDICTION
SYNDROME' WHISPERED THE DOCTOR

CONSTANCE GENEROUSLY OFFERED
TO HELP PENELOPE GET FRED TO
HIS DENTAL APPOINTMENT

ONCE OR TWICE A YEAR FRED GOT
TOGETHER WITH HIS OLD SCHOOL
PALS, 'BEAKY' BALDWIN, 'SMARMY'
SMITH AND 'EMBARRASSING' ED

AT LAST PENELOPE FOUND THE
PERFECT WAY TO KEEP FIT,
'VIRTUAL AEROBICS'

FRED AND PENELOPE FREQUENTLY
GOT LOST BETWEEN THE
KITCHEN AND THE LOUNGE

PENELOPE SOMETIMES WISHED FRED PUT
AS MUCH ENERGY INTO THEIR MARRIAGE
AS HE DID INTO HIS HOBBIES

ON THE FIRST DAY OF HIS NEW JOB
FRED EXPERIENCED A FEW
TEETHING PROBLEMS

FRED THOUGHT A LITTLE MUSIC
MIGHT SOOTHE PENELOPE'S MIGRAINE

FRED AND PENELOPE WERE NEVER
AT THEIR BEST FIRST THING
IN THE MORNING

'I THINK THEY CALL IT THE MALE MENOPAUSE,' WHISPERED PENELOPE

WITH REGULAR VISITS TO THE PET
CEMETERY FRED WAS GRADUALLY
COMING TO TERMS WITH THE
LOSS OF HIS ANT

FRED WAS DETERMINED TO PROVE THE
EXISTENCE OF THE MONSTER

WHEN IT CAME TO GARDENING
FRED AND PENELOPE MADE
A GREAT TEAM

FRED WAS DISAPPOINTED TO SEE A
TRUSTED FRIEND BREAKING THE RULES

FRED AND PENELOPE'S SKATING
PARTIES HAD BECOME A
POPULAR CHRISTMAS EVENT

PENELOPE THOUGHT SHE COULD DETECT
THE TELL-TALE SIGNS OF A
MID-LIFE CRISIS

FRED AND PENELOPE TRIED VARIOUS
WAYS OF MAKING THE WALK TO
THE LIBRARY MORE INTERESTING

24 HOUR NON-STOP EATATHON

CONSTANCE AND PENELOPE LIKED
TO DO THEIR BIT FOR CHARITY

FRED REALISED HE HAD MADE A
BIG MISTAKE BY CALLING
PENELOPE 'CUDDLY'

'HE'S FAILED TO MAKE THE HONOURS LIST AGAIN', SIGHED PENELOPE

FRED AND PENELOPE SENSED THAT
THIS WAS NO ORDINARY MOUSE

PENELOPE FINALLY DECIDED TO
DO SOMETHING ABOUT FRED'S
OVER-SLEEPING PROBLEM

FRED AND PIP SEEMED TO HAVE
BECOME A LOT CLOSER SINCE
PIP'S LOTTERY WIN

IT LOOKED LIKE IT WAS GOING
TO BE 'ONE OF THOSE DAYS'

FRED BELIEVED THERE WERE THREE
IMPORTANT WORDS IN COOKERY ;
PRESENTATION , PRESENTATION
AND PRESENTATION

PENELOPE SOMETIMES WISHED FRED
WOULD GET SOME NORMAL FRIENDS

FRED AND PENELOPE HAD ALWAYS
SENSED THAT BOB WOULD HAVE
LIKED TO HAVE BEEN MORE
THAN JUST A MILKMAN

IF THE TRUTH BE KNOWN, FRED
WAS SICK TO DEATH OF PENELOPE'S
GARDEN FURNITURE BURGERS

FRED FINALLY FINISHED THE
GRANNY ANNEXE

WHILE PENELOPE SERVED THE
HORS D'OEUVRES, FRED ENTERTAINED
THEIR GUESTS WITH THE STORY OF
HIS IN-GROWING TOE NAIL

AS THEY DEPARTED, FRED'S
GUESTS WERE EACH ISSUED WITH
A COMMEMORATIVE 'T' SHIRT

WHEN FRED AND PENELOPE SET OUT
FOR THEIR MEETING WITH THE LOCAL
PLANNING OFFICER IT WAS WITH
A SENSE OF FOREBODING

PENELOPE KINDLY AGREED TO ASSIST
FRED WITH RESEARCH FOR HIS
FORTHCOMING BOOK , 'A DAY IN THE
LIFE OF A ROLLING PIN'

FRED FOUND THAT BEING
HAUNTED WASN'T ALL BAD

PIP RELUCTANTLY AGREED TO ASSIST
FRED WITH THE TESTING OF HIS
LATEST INVENTION, AN AUTOMATED
NASAL HAIR REMOVER

PENELOPE HAD A TENDENCY TO
MONOPOLISE THE BISCUIT BARREL

FRED TOOK GREAT CARE TO ESTABLISH
THE PRECISE LOCATION OF HIS
MOTHER-IN-LAW'S HOUSE

IMELDA MARCOS HAD
NOTHING ON FRED

WHILE PENELOPE PREPARED THE DINNER
FRED LOOKED AFTER THE DRINKS

FRED COULDN'T HELP FEELING THAT
THE MILKMAN WAS BECOMING A
LITTLE OVER-FAMILIAR

FRED'S GOLF TECHNIQUE OWED A LOT
TO HIS GREAT SPORTING HERO,
ALEX 'HURRICANE' HIGGINS

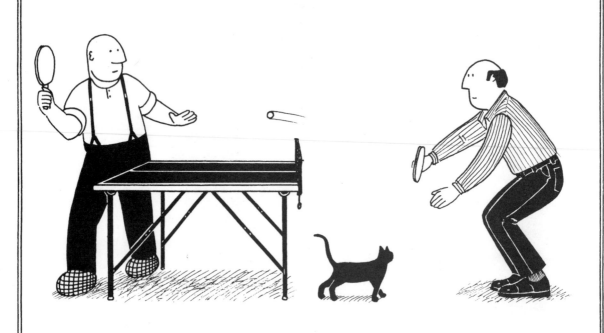

ON THE WEEKENDS FRED AND
PIP LIKED TO UNWIND WITH A
FEW GAMES OF PING

IT WAS ONE OF PENELOPE'S
'BAD HAIR' DAYS

FOR A SMALL FEE A FEW HAND-
PICKED INDIVIDUALS WERE ALLOWED
INTO THE HOUSE EACH MORNING
TO WATCH FRED EAT HIS PORRIDGE

IT WAS EARLY DAYS FOR FRED'S
POLITICAL CAREER

LIFE WITH FRED WAS FULL OF
THE UNEXPECTED

IT GAVE FRED IMMENSE SATISFACTION
TO RECALL PEOPLE'S SCORNFUL
LAUGHTER WHEN HE FIRST
PLANTED THE LIGHT BULB

PENELOPE COULDN'T HELP FEELING
THAT FRED WAS OVER-REACTING
TO THE GREENFLY

MONDAY WAS WASHDAY

PENELOPE WAS BECOMING CONCERNED
ABOUT FRED'S DRINKING

FRED AND PENELOPE FELT SURE THAT
BEFORE TOO LONG THE BANK MANAGER
WOULD BEGIN TO SEE THINGS
FROM THEIR POINT OF VIEW

IT WAS A COMFORT TO PENELOPE AND
FRED TO KNOW THAT IF EVER THEY FELL
UPON HARD TIMES THEY WOULD FETCH
A GOOD PRICE FOR GOD'S SLIPPERS

ONCE AGAIN THE SECRETARY OF THE
EXCLUSIVE 'POINTY HAT AND NOSE
CLUB' WAS FORCED TO REMIND PIP
OF THEIR STRICT DRESS CODE

FRED TOOK ADVANTAGE OF HIS FAMILY'S
CHRISTMAS VISIT TO CARRY OUT SOME
URGENT ROOF REPAIRS

'I BLAME ALL THOSE S.A.S. BOOKS
HE'S BEEN READING', SIGHED PENELOPE

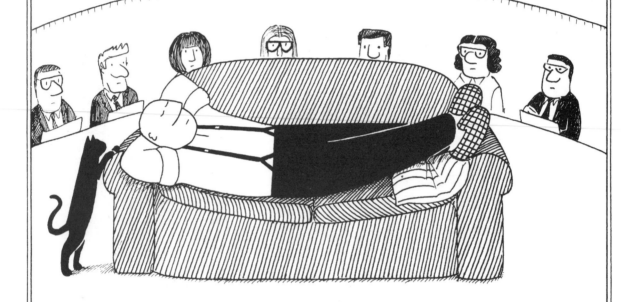

FRED WAS GOING FOR GOLD

HAVING OVERCOME THEIR INITIAL
SHYNESS FRED AND THE CREATURE
FROM THE DEEP FOUND THEY ACTUALLY
HAD QUITE A LOT IN COMMON

PENELOPE WAS DISMAYED TO SEE
FRED FIGHTING WITH THE
NEXT- DOOR NEIGHBOUR AGAIN

FRED AND PENELOPE'S NEW BATHROOM
MIRROR WAS GOING TO TAKE
SOME GETTING USED TO

IT WAS ANOTHER OF FRED'S
MOUNTAINEERING DREAMS

UNFORTUNATELY FOR FRED HIS ESCAPE
TUNNEL CAME UP SIX FEET SHORT
OF THE GARDEN FENCE

PENELOPE'S 'IT'S TEDDY OR ME' ULTIMATUM
APPEARED TO HAVE BACKFIRED

FRED HAD NEVER BEEN A GREAT
ONE FOR BIRTHDAY CELEBRATIONS

THE TROUBLE WITH HAVING MR AND MRS
JIGSAW AROUND WAS THAT ONE OF
THEM WOULD ALWAYS LOSE A PIECE

EVEN AS A BOY THE WORLD HAD
SEEMED STRANGE TO FRED

FRED FELT IT WAS TIME
FOR A CHANGE

IT WAS TIME FOR WALKIES

POPPING OVER TO THE NESBITS
FOR TEA AND SCONES WAS NEVER
QUITE AS SIMPLE AS IT SOUNDED

PENELOPE WAS NOT AT ALL
HAPPY WITH FRED'S PENCHANT
FOR VIRTUAL BATHS

FRED AND PENELOPE COULDN'T HELP
NOTICING THAT THE NEIGHBOURHOOD
WAS BECOMING MORE VIOLENT

HAVING VISITED LOURDES AND THE SHROUD
OF TURIN, FRED AND PENELOPE THEN
MADE A PILGRIMAGE TO THE LATEST BIG
ATTRACTION ON THE RELIGIOUS MAP

ABOUT TEN DAYS AFTER FRED'S VISIT
TO THE DOCTOR PENELOPE COULD
SENSE HIS ANTI-DEPRESSANTS
BEGINNING TO KICK IN

CONSIDERING FRED AND PENELOPE HAD
ONLY ATTENDED ONE YOGA CLASS
THEY WERE DOING WELL

PENELOPE WAS SURPRISED THAT :-
A. GOD HAD A WIFE , AND
B. SHE WAS SO VAIN

FRED AND PENELOPE WONDERED WHAT
HAD BECOME OF THEIR GUESTS SINCE THEY
FINISHED THEIR CHRISTMAS DINNER